Mae in the Middle
Music Master

Written by
Andrew Fusek Peters
and Polly Peters
Illustrated by
Finger Industries Ltd.

Contents

	Page
Chapter 1 Musical Goosebumps	4
Chapter 2 Music Fairies	9
Chapter 3 Practice Makes Perfect!	12
Chapter 4 A Close Call	20
Chapter 5 A Big Surprise	26

Chapter 1
Musical Goosebumps

At breakfast, Mae watched her younger sister pour the last of the cornflakes into her bowl.

"Hey, leave some for me!" said Mae.

"Mum says I need a good breakfast to start the day," Roz whined.

Mae's older brother, Alec, hid behind a maths book. He was slurping his orange juice noisily.

"Do you mind?" asked Mae. "That's disgusting."

Alec didn't mind at all. His friends called him Smart-Alec. He was a boy with a bright future.

At that moment, the radio announced an old tune by Miles Davis called *So What?*

As the music started, Alec looked up. "So what? That's exactly what I think!" he muttered.

As Mae listened, the music gave her goosebumps. It certainly beat anything in the charts!

"Mum?" asked Mae.

"What, darling?" Mum was busy making sandwiches and finding lunch money for Alec.

"What's that person playing?"

"Who? Oh, a trumpet, I think. Now Roz, have you found your socks or are you going to school barefoot?"

"I'd love to learn to play like that," sighed Mae.

"I'm sure you would," said Mum, "but we don't have time to think about lessons now. If you daydream any more, you'll be late for school."

"But Mum! Alec has computer club and Roz goes to dance class."

"Yes, and I'm rushed off my feet!" said Mum, kissing Mae on the forehead. "Put your plate in the dishwasher."

Mae frowned as the radio was switched off.

Chapter 2
Music Fairies

Mae was silent all the way to school, but Mum didn't notice. The tune from the radio went round in Mae's head.

It was like being haunted by …

a musical ghost.

"Off with the fairies again?" Mae's best friend Asha asked her at break time.

"Yes! Music fairies!" Mae laughed.

"What are you on about?" Asha looked puzzled.

"I heard someone playing a trumpet on the radio. It was amazing!"

"Oh, that thing. My sister drives us mad practising on hers!" Asha rolled her eyes. "The same tunes, over and over."

Mae looked up, excited. She had forgotten that Asha's older sister, Meera, played in the school band.

"I wish I could play the trumpet at the school concert. How difficult is it to learn?"

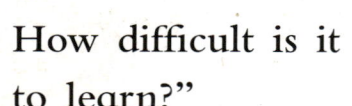

Asha shrugged. "It's no use asking me. You need to ask Meera."

Mae smiled. "Great idea, Asha! How about after school?"

Asha grinned too. "I don't suppose you'll stop going on about it otherwise!"

Chapter 3
Practice Makes Perfect!

"Mum, can I play at Asha's house?"

Mum was outside school, still waiting for Roz to come out. She was looking at her watch. "OK, but I need to pick you up at six o'clock sharp."

"Thanks, Mum!" Mae raced off to catch up with her friend.

Half an hour later, Meera walked in with an odd-shaped case.

"Is that your trumpet?" Mae asked. She stared at the case as if it were a priceless painting.

"It is. You should hear how good it sounds," said Meera, proudly.

Mae looked longingly at the trumpet. She reached out to touch it. "Would you let me have a go?" she said, nervously.

Meera smiled. "Come on then. Let's go outside. We can be noisy there!"

Mae couldn't wait to hold the trumpet, but first Meera explained about the different parts.

Meera put the trumpet into Mae's left hand. She showed Mae how to rest her right hand on the finger valves. Mae put the mouthpiece to her lips and blew. It sounded like a squawking bird! Meera just laughed and told Mae to have another go.

Mae concentrated on making her mouth into the right shape, and this time there was a long, clear sound.

Meera beamed. "Some people just pick it up straight away," she told Mae. "You're lucky, but to play a tune takes hard work and practice. Would you like me to teach you?"

Mae couldn't believe her luck. Over the next eight weeks she spent even more time than usual at Asha's house. She didn't say a word about the trumpet to her mum, Roz or Alec. She wanted it to be a surprise when she played at the school concert.

Chapter 4
A Close Call

Asha was busy drawing while Meera told Mae to keep playing the same notes again and again.

"So, how is she doing?" Asha asked her sister.

"Brilliantly!" said Meera. "Mae is a natural. It's great to see her improving so quickly."

Asha's dad came into the sitting room. "Well done with the teaching, Meera," he said. "Now then, how about a tune, young Mae?"

Mae turned red. The school concert was only a week away. She wasn't sure if she was ready. "OK, Mr Gupta. If you insist!"

Mr Gupta laughed. "I do. We can call it payment for all that cake you've eaten!"

Mae lifted the trumpet. She was nervous, but the moment she put the instrument to her lips and closed her eyes ...

... a beautiful tune filled the room.

Suddenly, the doorbell rang. A figure stood behind the frosted glass.

Oh no! It was Mae's mum. Mae thrust the trumpet back into Meera's hands.

Mae's mum came rushing in. "Goodness, your playing is impressive, Meera! That sounded great."

Mae tried not to smile. What a close call that had been!

"Hurry up, Mae. Alec needs to be picked up from computer club and I'm running late, again."

Chapter 5
A Big Surprise

It was the end of term concert and the school hall was packed. Mae's mum arrived late. Mae could see her standing at the back.

The infants went first, with a short play about animals. They banged drums and Roz shook a tambourine as the class did a dance.

Next came the recorders. Mae's mouth was dry and her heart beat loudly.

"And now," said Mrs Miggins, "we have a special treat. This girl here has been working very hard, so give her a big clap!"

crowd. She could imagine Alec making faces at her. Her fingers were sweaty and Meera's trumpet felt heavy. She tried not to look at her mum. It was just as well because her mum's mouth had dropped open!

Mae wiggled her fingers and closed her lips in determination. It was now or never. The first note squeaked out. Mae almost gave up, but she looked up and saw Meera smiling.

The second note was better. The tune flowed out and filled the hall.

Suddenly, the audience erupted. No one clapped louder than Mae's mum. Even Alec looked impressed.

After the concert finished, Mae's mum gave her a big hug. "Oh Mae! If this is the kind of thing you get up to behind my back, I'll be happy forever! Next term, we'll find time for lessons, I promise!"

Mae beamed. Maybe it wasn't so bad being Mae in the Middle after all.

At the end, there was a silence. Mae's face fell. Had she done badly?